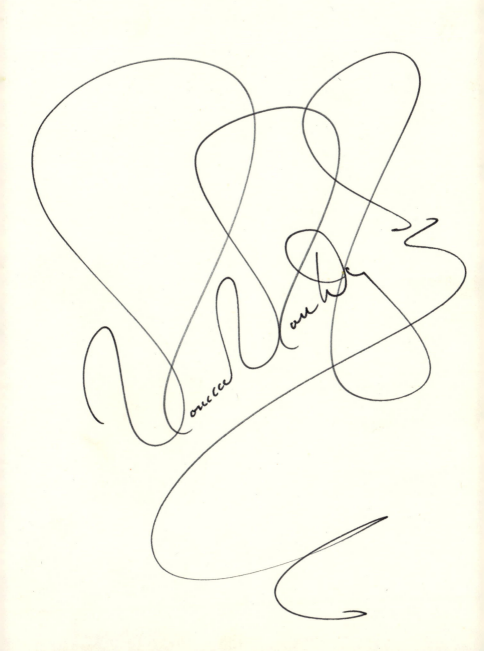

W9-CCF-911

Your Love Is Here

Books by *Vonda Van Dyke*

That Girl in Your Mirror
Dear Vonda Kay
Reach Up

Your Love Is Here

All pictures and lettering done by me!

Vonda Van Dyke

Doubleday & Company, Inc.

Garden City, New York

1974

ISBN 0-385-09539-2
Library of Congress Catalog Card Number 74-3699
Copyright © 1974 by Vonda Van Dyke
All Rights Reserved
Printed in the United States of America
First Edition

The lyrics from "Be With Me" and "All This and Heaven Too" are used with the permission of Miss "A" Publishing Co.

"Our Lord's Prayer" © copyright 1972 by Word Music, Inc. All rights reserved. "Gonna Love" © copyright 1971 by Word Music, Inc. All rights reserved. Used by permission.

This is

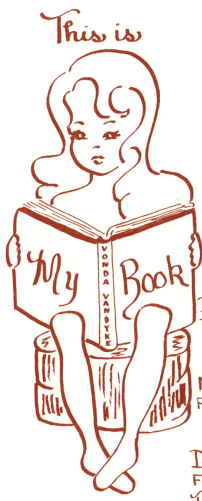

My Book

VONDA VANDYKE

BUT I'D REALLY LIKE TO TAKE
TIME TO ESPECIALLY THANK.

MOM & DAD
For the talents I inherited

and

DICK SHACK
For guiding me
Into developing them.

DOUBLEDAY
For feeling they merited
Publishing.

~ Introduction ~

Well, here we are again **LORD**
I always end up talking to You
About everything.

In our little talks it seems,
I learn a lot about me.
I question, I argue,
I rebel, and I agree
I bring up problems 'bout
Friends & enemies

You've noticed,
When I talk to you,
I don't use "Thee" or "Thou"
I do have respect
It's just that,
It's also true,
You seem like a Friend.
You're a very Important Friend
In fact,
You're the MOST important Friend
That I have.

I read Your book
Over and over again.
And some of the things
I learn, and re-learn

I bring up with You
As I pray now and then.
You're very patient to listen
Especially when my ideas
And discoveries
Must seem to You
Not too profound.

Talking with You is like
Visiting with no one else
I'm not as honest with anyone
I'm not even as honest with myself
When I haven't invited
You to listen in.

I just want you to know though.
I really feel You.
And You really help me.
And Your presence is something
I really need
Very much!

Thanks for being there
Thank You most of all for caring!

YOUR LOVE IS HERE

I feel it.

It wraps itself
around me

It surges deep
inside me.

Please let it spring up

And flow to others!

Be with me Father,
I need no other
Than You,
To see me through
Until tomorrow.

Help me to bury
My Sorrow.

Teach me to reach
For Your peace.

Help me to borrow
Your love,
And give it away

To
EVERYONE

I meet
today!

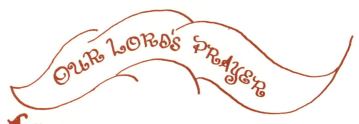

OUR LORD'S PRAYER

Father,
How respected and honored
Is Your name
Let us live for the kingdom
That will soon
Be ours to claim.

May we always do Your will
While we're here on earth,
Just like it's done in heaven.

Give us this day,
Supply all our needs,
Help us to forgive our brother's
Wrong deeds.
As You forgive us.

Don't let us bow to sin
As we walk along life's road.
Keep our heads held high,
And keep our eyes
Always on You.

May Your kingdom dwell within us.
May Your power make us strong.
May Your glory reign forever!

It's early in the mornin'
It's dark and no one's movin'
In the city.

You can feel it gettin' ready
To be day.

That's the time thats best,
The time when the rest
Of the world is asleep.

Thats the time when
There's a quiet time
To pray.

Problems have to BUILD UP
Before they

BLOW UP

So please,
Remind me to discuss
All the things that disgust me

BEFORE
they

ERUPT

Into something I'm sorry for.

Hey Lord!

Would ya look at me?
I'm really flyin' high today!
I woke up SOOOOOOOOO
Happy!

Now my day has just begun
And something or someone
May come
And try to spoil it!
Please keep in mind
That I'm flying
And pretty high!
Could you help me stay up
Without crashing?
(Just for today?)

I'd like my new found high
To last.
'Cause in the past
I've not always 'wakened this way!

Lord, I expected
    The SUN to shine today.
Lord, I never thought
    I'd be cryin' in the rain.

LORD, I just can't make it
Through this storm myself.
If I'm ever gonna' live to see
The sun tomorrow,
    'GONNA HAVE TO HAVE
    A LOT OF YOUR HELP!

Sometimes
I'm a

THRILL
SEEKER

But thrills often
lead to spills!

Help me,
To be sometimes satisfied
With the ordinary.
So I can avoid the dangers
Of the extraordinary.

I'm making plans
I'm working
I'm trying
Perfecting

But the outcome of my labor has
To be placed
In Your hands.
Without You in it
Success would have no meaning.

As a father,
  Knowing I'm your child

must drive you up the wall

                    Sometimes!

But,
  Thanks for assuring me
That because I was born
Into your family;
You love me
        And wanna' keep me!

Sometimes
my heart breaks
too easily.

I take things
too seriously.

I accept things
too emotionally.

Help me to
Cool it!

She says:

thanks for making me so humble

'Cause I'm darn proud of it!

Thanks For Friends

True friends
Are those who can express
Their feelings, thoughts
And reactions honestly

There aren't many around like that

But somehow,
You manage to send them to me

Just when they're needed most!

You're invited to: Come into my life

time: now

place: right where I am

reason: I just can't make it by myself!

🌼 RSVP requested

At times
I get to running
So fast that I
Can't Remember
Where I'm running
Or why!

When my feet
Are constantly
In motion, they
Must be hard
For You to
Guide.

"We
from crying over
yesterday's hurts,
So I can begin
Living Today
for
Tomorrow!

You light
All the dark corners of my mind.

You rescue me
From the treacherous sea
of doubt:
That sometimes
Engulfs my thoughts.

Many times I could
Be accused of
Keeping my **love**
In a beautiful locked box.
Telling everyone
How much I've got,
But never showing it
To anyone
And never taking it out
To give to someone.

Please break the lock
And throw away the key.
Help me to be as free
In giving love to others
As you are in
Giving love to me.

I CAN'T SWIM
NOT IN THE
TROUBLED SEA
I'M IN!

NOW I LAY ME DOWN TO SLEEP

I PRAY THE LORD MY SOUL TO KEEP

IF I SHOULD DIE BEFORE I WAKE

Better
I should wake
before I die
and find
how I might better
LIVE

It's rush, rush, rush,
Then suddenly it's over.
The day is done.
It becomes quiet & hushed
Then...
I soak up restful hours
like a sponge.
Knowing tomorrow
will SQUEEZE me dry
and I
will race the clock
Until it's time
To rest again.

Lord, I guess you see
the rut I'm in!

Please show me
how to begin
to walk life at a
slower pace
So I'll have time
To enjoy it!

I WAS ON MY WAY OUT OF MY MIND.

Oh God!
My whole brain got clogged.
I was so worried,
So upset,
So confused,
That I couldn't think or even pray!
I felt like hell couldn't last
As long as that day!

But it's tomorrow now
And some how,
Thanks to You my Friend,
I've managed
To get it all together again!

If the words of the song
be RIGHT
Please help me not to
criticize
The style of the man
who sings them.

Sometimes I wonder
If this old world will ever
Patch up all its differences
And get together.

In a world that's ours to share,
For us to know real peace,
It's gonna' take a lotta love.

Help it to begin

With me!

Never let me reach the point
of saying

"is that
all there
is"

'Cause If I ever do
I'll be no good to me
Or to You!

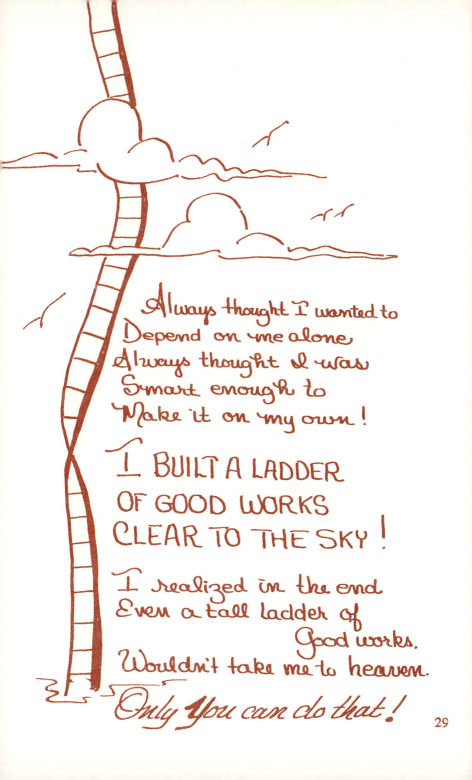

Always thought I wanted to
Depend on me alone,
Always thought I was
Smart enough to
Make it on my own!

I BUILT A LADDER
OF GOOD WORKS
CLEAR TO THE SKY!

I realized in the end
Even a tall ladder of
          Good works.
Wouldn't take me to heaven.
Only You can do that!

29

If

SUCCESS

were my only aim

and

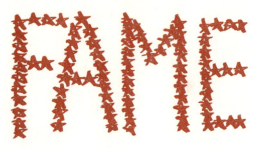

FAME

MY ONLY GOAL

I'd die like everyone else... ALONE!

PM

Beans!
I'm sick of schedules
I hate this rat race
I'm tired of this hectic pace
I can no longer compete
I'm pooped ... I'm Beat!
This is it! I QUIT!

AM

Now that I've had
a good night's sleep

I'm not ready to meet defeat
I'm ready to get in there & fight.
FORGET WHAT I SAID LAST NIGHT!

Dear Brothers,
Is your life full of dif-
ficulties and temptations? Then
Be happy, for when the way is
rough, your patience has a chance
to grow. So let it grow, and
don't try to squirm out of your
problems. For when your patience
is finally in full bloom, then
you will be ready for anything,
strong in character, full and
complete.   James 1:2-4

How long does patience take
To reach it's fullest bloom?
It's grown a lot, I know,
But, how long does it
Have to grow?

I've tried to live happily
And face each day
The way You've asked,
Meeting head-on my problems,
Hoping at last
To be strong, complete
And full,

But, perhaps I'll never be.
'Cause I tend to get discouraged.
'Cause I'm one of the weak.
Who needs
To lean on You!

Where have all the flowers gone ?

My mind seems
to be
Only growing weeds.

What I need
Is for You to come along
And pull up the weeds
And replant flowers.

Hey "life mender"

See what you can do,
With this life that I've messed up.
With what you've got to work with,
It should be quite a test of
Your power and love!

You're

It's reassuring
Knowing when life's sea

Is churning
You'll be there to keep me
Where I should be.

It seems we want
to use up everything!
The sky
    The air
        The oil

We spoil all we touch,
And seem to not much care.

Are we thinking
        It's Your job to repair it?
Are we assuming,
    If we go on ruining,
You'll just
        give us a new one?

I wake up almost every mornin'
Sayin' it's GREAT to be alive,
The beauty of your presence
I can never quite describe
BUT I'LL KEEP TRYING!

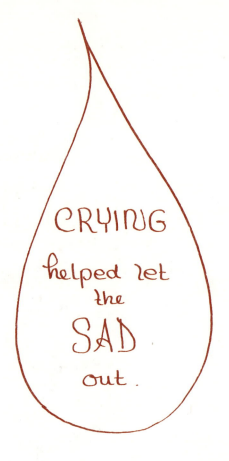

CRYING

helped let the

SAD

out.

Now if You don't mind
I really think it's time
You put some HAPPY in!

LOVE is WHEN
I can REACH OUT for
others
and
REALLY FEEL THEM
Help me to
do that more!

At the end of my day
I need time to get away.
I need time to be alone.
Time when I can share
All my problems, plans & hopes
With someone who CARES

After my busy day
You're like the quiet feel of slumber.
Like, after the sun of summer,
You're the welcome feel of fall.

You've shown me
That if there be
Only a twig of hope
Left upon life's tree
I should
   Perch myself on it!

44

She sings,

She smiles,

She does nice things

For everyone.

She's always busy.

Always giving.

But,

She must have needs too!
Make me more sensitive
Show me what I can do
For her!

I've watched palm trees
Sway to the whispered song
Of an ocean's gentle breeze.
I've seen the intricate design of a snowflake
And once in a while I take
Time to wonder at a rainbow
As it bridges heaven to earth
Or marvel at a red sky
As it was giving birth
To a new day.
I've climbed the purple colored mountains
And waded in crystal rivers
And floated aimlessly on glassy lakes.

HOW COULD YOU CREATE SOMETHING SO BEAUTIFUL
FOR US WHO SEEM TO CARE SO LITTLE?

"FORGET THE PAST"?

What good is it
To file knowledge away
If I never take it out
And use it again?

I seem to go on making
The same mistakes
So what good is experience when
I don't learn from it?

Please don't allow me
To forget my past.
Rather, help me to use it!

WHEN YOU'RE AT THE WHEEL
I'M SAFE,

But then, I can't wait
To get my hands back on it again.

That's when things get rough.
That's when I CRACK UP.
That's when accidents happen!

Peace

is
when you put
my
TURMOIL
in
Repose.

Dear God,

Thanks for letting me have You as a Friend.
From your friendship I've learned how to love others.
You've shown me, how best to be, a brother to everyone.
Regardless of their habits beliefs or color.

Thanks.

Love Always.
Y?

"Prayer Changes Things"

But mostly,
it
Changes me!

What's the big deal about New Year's?

Can't people start over
On other days
Than Jan 1st?
How about May 3d?
What's wrong with November 13th
Or September 17th
With the striking of each new midnight
We have the opportunity to begin
A new and different life,
But, we don't!

That's 'cause we keep trying
To change all by ourselves
When will we learn
That we need **Your** help?

Money is such a pressure
Because people have set it up
As a true measure
of
VALUE and SUCCESS

How do I tell them that I feel
That my real success and value
lies in the amount of faith I have in You?

LOVE OTHERS

AS MYSELF

HUH?

I've been workin at that,
But, It ain't been easy!

For strangers I have tolerance
For loved ones I have patience.
But with myself?
I get exasperated!
I can't seem to
Reach far enough,
Stand tall enough,
Move fast enough,
Or speak up loud enough!
But .....

If I were satisfied,
Then I wouldn't have to try,
And life? ......

(Would be pretty dull!)

I have a young friend
Who makes up for her lack of
Wisdom, experience & maturity
By being what grown-ups
Find it hard to be.
Honest!

She's a big help.
Often the judgement of someone else
Is flavored with tact
But I always know
My shrewd young friend
Will give me only fact.

When she grows up,
Please keep her like that!

God,
Lots of times
It's really hard knowin',
If what I'm doin'
Is right!

It's not like you write
In cloud capped letters
Cross the sky —

RIGHT ON BROTHER

(In fact you probably wouldn't write that!)

I know,
You gave me a good mind,
And a conscience to rely on.
But still a little sign, now & then
Would be helpful in the long run!

Come to think of it,
Knowing You and Your concern
I wouldn't be a bit surprised to learn
That .....
THE SIGNS HAVE BEEN THERE
AND I'VE JUST BEEN MISSING THEM!

Open my eyes
That I might see

THE BAD,
as well as
THE GOOD
in me!

Slammed the door
Once more!
We disagreed
Now I feel like
You're tellin' ME
To patch it up!

Well, I don't think
I can!
I've had enough!
WHY do I
Have to be the one
To say I'm sorry?

Just 'cause
I'm the one who's
Wrong again?

I LOVE YOU, GOD!
But why did ya' have ta'
Send me this one?
She's got lots of problems
But why does she always come to me?
I'm really so busy!
Now You know, I always love to help.
But this is gettin' a bit "draggie".

I'm not that bright or that wise
And my answers aren't all that bright!
(Although if I go on completely seeking
Your guidance they should be.)

.OK! You win! I agree!
I'm the best one for her to see.

SO
~~BUT~~ PLEASE

Help me to be patient.
Help me to show her how to learn
To begin taking some of her
Problems to YOU!

You said,

"Be thankful for everything."

I'm sure that You're aware
That sometimes that's hard for me!

When PROBLEMS rain down

And my SUN doesn't shine,

I FORGET TO BE THANKFUL

BUT. FROM NOW ON I'll TRY!

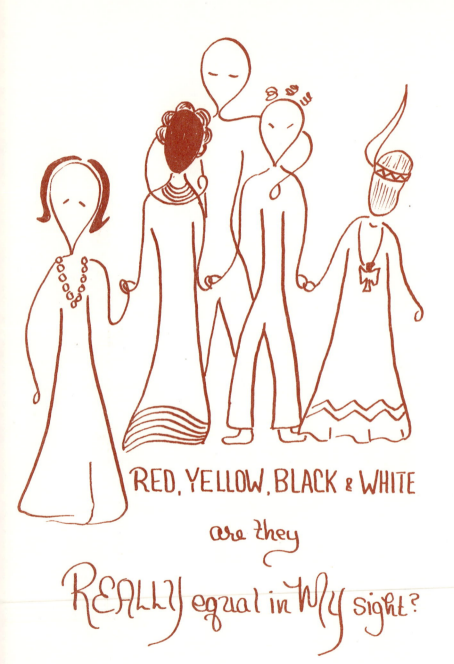

RED, YELLOW, BLACK & WHITE

are they

REALLY equal in MY sight?

Why do people argue
Fight and even hate?
Why do they march off to war
Not as Christian soldiers
But as criticizers of
Anothers faith
How come we turn away
Someone who you love
Because
Of a denomination
Or an interpretation
When will we discover
That You're the Father
And it's Your job to
Decide who's a brother
And not ours?

My friend called;
Her father died.
And I didn't know
What to say
Words seem so empty
When someone you care about
Is in pain.
All I could think to tell her
Was that I'd pray.
I'll be honest with you God,
Even that didn't seem like enough!

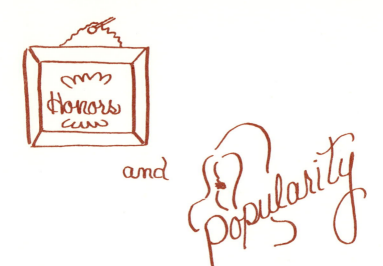

Honors

and Popularity

Only lead to
HARD FEELINGS
and
Jealousy

So why do we
So conscientiously
Try to please EVERYONE?

Everyone BUT you!

Show me
That I'm loved
Show me
That You care
if
You're up above
if
You're there
Somewhere.

Hey "Super Doc",

Today my confidence
is shaggy

My thought
waves have

got the FRIZZIES

Generally my mind is sickly.

Can you do something?

Rx Perhaps a change of attitude?
A fresh new outlook?
(Any old miracle will do!)

Why all the time
keep asking

WHY

Shouldn't I
be asking
WHAT
WHERE
HOW
?

God,
Sometimes when I pray
It doesn't feel like You're listening.
I know You're always there,
'Cause You said You would be

But, I STILL DOUBT sometimes!

Especially
When I think,

"How small I am
AND HOW BIG
YOU ARE."

Why should you even care?
Oh, I guess "why" isn't important.
The important thing is that You do!

Thank You!

If

At first I don't

succeed

God,

Give me

Strength.

Lord,
  I remember not long ago
I was afraid of being alone.
I'd pick up the phone
And call anyone I knew
Just to make it through
An evening by myself.
I hated the loneliness!
So I called on you for help.
I guess you didn't hear me.
Or did you?
  The most amazing
              thing happened

  I discovered
That I had a need
Not to fill my time with company
But to take and use
The time alone
To get to know & discover me!

Know what's nice?
  That silent moment
Before I fall asleep at night.
  I feel SECURE.
  I feel ASSURED.
That YOU love me,
No matter what I've done
To disappoint you!

Everything we learn or gain,
Everything we seek or obtain,
Depends on your gift of time.
Help us to ambitiously use
Each moment you give us
of life.

No crown will ever be
As important as the one
I'll someday receive.

The crown of life

The one you give
To those who live & believe
As you
Ask them to.

Teach
me to try
To live my Life
Just
One day at
a
Time

When I got impatient
My daddy used to say
"It's just over the next hill.
It's just around the next bend."
   (But it wouldn't be there.)
And we'd keep driving for miles on end

That's the way my life seems to be
But I keep pushing on expectantly
I know you've got something
Great for me!
      But, where is it?
      How far away?
You say ----

"It's just over the next hill?
It's just around the next bend?"

Well ok then ---I BELIEVE YOU!

You said that I could
          Move a mountain
If I had faith the size
Of a little mustard seed.
I really don't believe
I've got that much faith.
(I feel like I've got more)
But I must not 'cause
A mountain still looks
          awfully Big!

You're so

Boldly aggressive

so

UNFALTERINGLY

SECURE

So Marvelously

SENSITIVE

Can't you make me
just a little that way?

Your love is beautiful

Thanks for showing it to me.

Thanks for giving it so freely.

Thanks for letting me share it,
Even though I don't deserve to
Thanks for saying, when the world
Turns against me.

" You're mine and

I
Love
You "

Thanks for filling my moments of loneliness
With Your presence.
Thank You for squelching all my doubts
With Your promises.

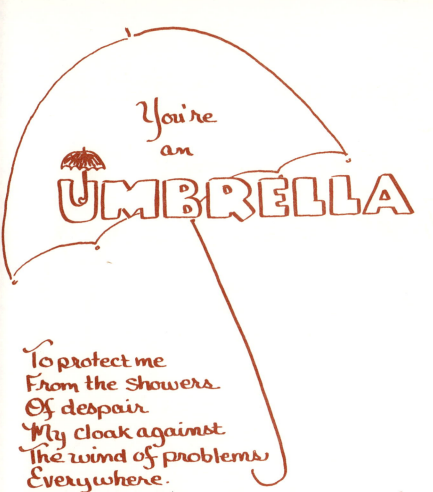

You're
an
UMBRELLA

To protect me
From the showers.
Of despair
My cloak against
The wind of problems
Everywhere.
My shield against the cutting words
That people sometimes say

My RAINBOW that promises
A bright and sunny day!

83

Don't let me be
Just another painted personality
Colored exactly as I'd like to be.
Don't let me put on a plastic face
A carbon copy of a manufactured race.
Don't let me lose my identity.
Don't let me wish to be someone else.
Help me to be happy with myself.
Don't let me be like those I meet.
KEEP ME UNIQUE
And thankful to remain
The personality you created me.

Life is
Hills & Valleys!

A mile
of mountain top
feeling.

Followed
closely by miles
of feeling low.

But thanks.
for giving us both!

Without one
We might not be able
To appreciate the other!

Thanks for loaning me the world for a while
I really appreciate what it has
I enjoy it a lot, and will as long as it lasts.

    You've given me more on earth
    Much more than I deserve.
    Help me to use my life
    And all Your blessings
    To serve You. well!

DON'T LET ME USE MY RELIGION AS A FENCE
TO PROTECT ME AGAINST

The world and the people
Around me.

Rather,

Let
me
use
my
faith

as a bridge.

To take

me to other people,
and other people to Thee.

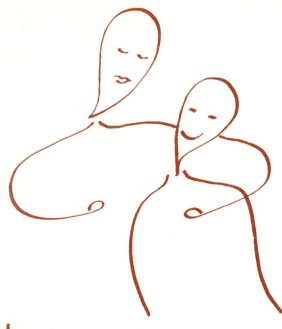

YOU said,
Don't pretend to love others
Really love them!
But, what about when
You find someone
You just <u>can't</u> love?
Isn't it alright to pretend them?
'Cause sometimes when I pretend
It often happens in the end
That I learn to at least like them!

Please
don't
cut me off!

Even when I'm sometimes slow
At getting to know
How You want things done.

Lord above,
You know
What this day will bring
Whether I will cry
Whether I will sing
Whether I will rise
To meet my brother's needs,
Whether I will sow
Your seeds of love.

I'm a
Child of God.

Yea!

'Cause now every day

that I feel INSIGNIFICANT,

Knowing I belong to You,

will make me feel IMPORTANT!

I'm standing at the edge of morning.
Knowing that with the sun
It's sure to come
Another day — with a new chance
To find a way To please You!

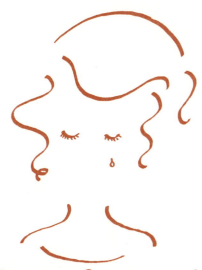

The other day I really got hurt.
Someone embarrassed me
Quite unecessarily
I sat there like a trooper and silently
Took nearly all that I could take
Realizing that she
Had a greater need
To put me down
Than I had to retaliate.
So I didn't try to get back at her.
That's good!
But I haven't forgotten
Or forgiven either.
I guess I should,
But I can't!
You'll have to help me with that!

Every once in a while
We meet someone we can't forget
Someone who remains in our minds
Like a lovely island
In the sea of people we've met.
What draws us to some people
What makes us feel
Like we want to be friends?
Did you give us a special radar
To equip us to tune in
On the people who are
To be special in our lives?
Do you guide us to the ones
Who'll become
Meaningful to us?
You must!

'Cause I couldn't have rounded up
Such a beautiful bunch
Of friends myself!

Thanks

for the

*Liberator

*John 3:16

Have You noticed
How I waste so much time
Trying to save it?

(Does that bug you?
     Well, It bugs me too!)

Lord,
I thought **I** was too big
For little things
But as always You knew
The real truth.
   When I became honest
   I also got wise,
   And realized......

   If I think I'm too BIG
   for the little things,

   I'm too little
for the BIG ones!

It's so still
All I hear is water
            brushing sand.
It sounds and looks
like Your mighty hand
Anointing the earth
            with peace.

Some people are twinkling stars in the sky *
* * * * * * * * * * * * * * *
* Pointing the way to where you abide.

Others are like SEARCHLIGHTS

helping others through their night.

Some are like

BEACONS

Guiding the lost ones.

THAT'S ME!
(JUST A LITTLE CANDLE!)
* You can use me too, can't you?

* MATT 5:16

102

I've closed all the doors
of my mind
To everything that
has upset me.

Now can you open
The portholes of my soul
To accept your beautiful

PEACE?

There is something
In my life
That shouldn't
Be there, I know.
But, I don't really
Want it to go.
It's wrong,
But I won't ask you
To take it from me.
Because it means too much!
I know, my priorities
Are all mixed up.
So, what can I say?
What can I ask?
That you take the desire
To continue the wrong away?
Well, if you can do that,
(Which you probably can)
Then, and only then,
Can I give it up!

104

RING THE BELLS

MAJOR BREAKTHROUGH

I finally did something the way *You* wanted me to!

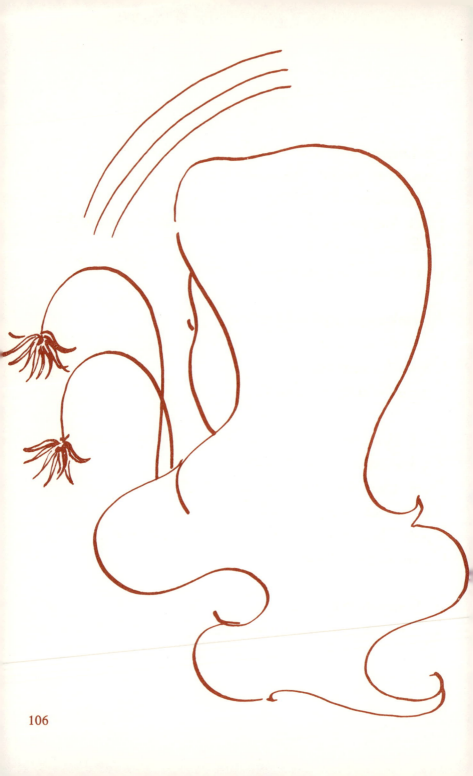

Outside my window
Was the most beautiful sunset
I wanted to keep it forever
But before I could even get a camera
It had passed.
How come beautiful things don't last?

Rainbows disappear
Flowers wilt
Cloud castles blow away
Snowflakes melt.

Did You mean for it to be that way?
If beauty could stay
Did You think we'd forget
It was special?
Did You think it could become
Commonplace?

(Knowing us
It probably would!)

"Gonna' love my enemies.
Gonna' do good to those
Who are bad to me.
I'm gonna' love with a love
That has no bias.
Love with a love that
Has no prejudice."

If You'll show me how

I'll start right now!

If I let my roots
Grow deep into
The soil of Your love,
I can stand up
Against the storm,
Knowing I'm secure,
I can reach out
With love and peace
Even to a world torn
By hate and war.

Yesterday

I cannot relive.

Today

is

All I have to work with.
Help me to do some thing
really great with it!

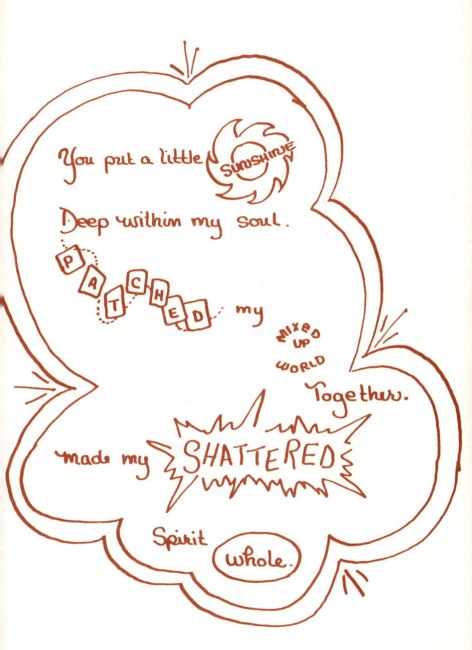

You put a little SUNSHINE

Deep within my soul.

PATCHED my

MIXED UP WORLD

Together.

made my SHATTERED

Spirit whole.

Sometimes I think

A loss

Comes along,

To show me who's boss

But You
Show me who's in charge too,
When I'm a winner
'Cause I'm always aware
That I couldn't have done it

Without You!

Help me to learn to tell others of your love for them and help me to be ready when a brother needs a friend

I've gone with the wind

I seem to be
Lost again!

Help me find
my way back
One more time!

Right now, I feel happy inside
I'm not really sure why
Nothing really great happened today
To make me feel this way!

It may just be a New Awareness
And a deep feeling of Thankfulness
For All You've done
And will do!

I went to church last Sunday
And as I walked inside the door
It felt like someone's
Arms wrapped around me.

Maybe it was You
Maybe it was
Your Spirit working through
The people there.

But, it was a beautiful feeling,
The feeling that You and they
Both cared.

This is

THE END

of my book

But thank You for assuring
There will never be an ending
to Your

LOVE
!